```
. . . . . . . . . . . . . . . . . . . . . . . . . . . . . . . . . . . .
.                                                                     .
.                                                                     .
.                                                                     .
.                                                                     .
.                                                                     .
.                                                                     .
.                       Place photo here                              .
.                                                                     .
.                                                                     .
.                                                                     .
.                                                                     .
.                                                                     .
. . . . . . . . . . . . . . . . . . . . . . . . . . . . . . . . . . . .
```

A photo of my family

FREDERICK WARNE
Published by the Penguin Group
Penguin Books Ltd, 80 Strand, London WC2R 0RL, England
Penguin Young Readers Group, 345 Hudson Street, New York, New York 10014, USA
Penguin Group (Canada), 90 Eglinton Avenue East, Suite 700, Toronto, Ontario, Canada M4P 2Y3
Penguin Ireland, 25 St Stephen's Green, Dublin 2, Ireland
Penguin Group (Australia), 250 Camberwell Road, Camberwell, Victoria 3124, Australia
Penguin Books India (P) Ltd, 11 Community Centre, Panchsheel Park, New Delhi 110 017, India
Penguin Group (NZ), 67 Apollo Drive, Rosedale, North Shore 0632, New Zealand
Penguin Books (South Africa) (Pty) Ltd, P O Box 9, Parklands 2121, South Africa
Penguin Books Ltd, Registered Offices: 80 Strand, London WC2R 0RL, England
Website: www.peterrabbit.com
First published by Frederick Warne 2008
1 3 5 7 9 10 8 6 4 2
Copyright © Frederick Warne & Co., 2008
Frederick Warne & Co. is the owner of all rights, copyrights and
trademarks in the Beatrix Potter character names and illustrations.

ISBN 978 0 7232 6284 8
Illustrations by Liz Catchpole
Printed in Italy

The Peter Rabbit Naturally Better initiative promotes ethical and
environmentally-friendly methods of manufacture. This book is printed
using vegetable inks, on chlorine-free and acid-free paper made from
responsibly managed sources certifed by the Forestry Stewardship Council.

Mixed Sources
Product group from well-managed
forests, controlled sources and
recycled wood or fiber
www.fsc.org Cert no. SA-COC-1592
© 1996 Forest Stewardship Council

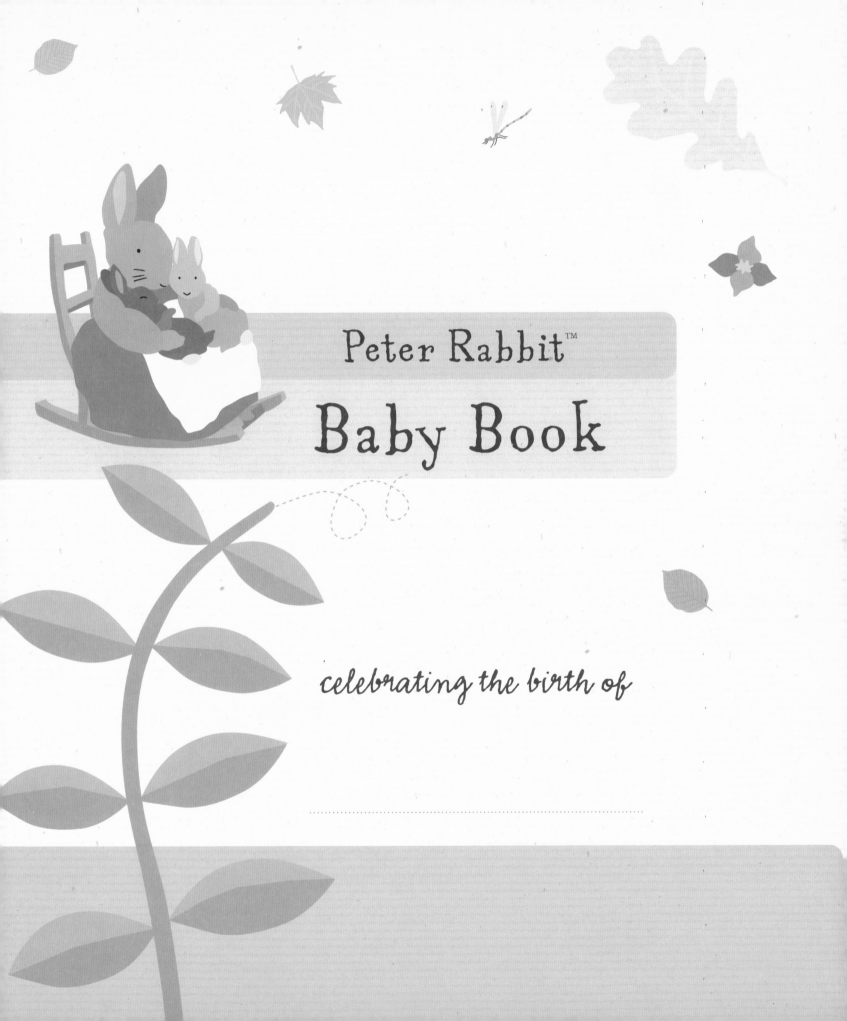

Peter Rabbit™
Baby Book

celebrating the birth of

....

Waiting for you
Our baby is on the way

We first knew you were coming on ....

The first time we felt you move ....

We first heard your heartbeat on ....

Our thoughts on knowing you are going to arrive

....

....

....

....

Our hopes for you in the future

....

....

....

....

....

....

....

....

....

....

Getting ready for you
preparations for our new arrival

This is a picture
of your nursery

Place photo here

Some of the new
things we bought
for you

....

....

....

....

Some of the things we were given or lent

. . . .

. . . .

Some special things in your room

. . . .

. . . .

. . . .

This is what we can see outside your nursery window

Place photo here

Finding out about you
The date gets closer

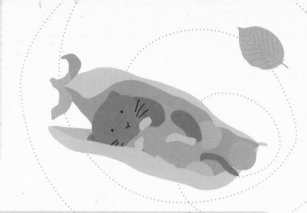

Prenatal appointments

Date ....

Date ....

Date ....

Names of doctors
or midwives who
looked after us

....

....

....

Notes and memories of our early visits to the hospital or clinic

....

....

All about our sonogram

....

....

Date you were due ....

Place sonogram photo here

Your birth day
A wonderful new life begins

Where we were when we knew you were on your way

....
....
....
....
....

Date you were born ....

Time you were born ....

You weighed ....

You measured ....

Your eyes were ....

City and state in which you were born

....

....

The name of the hospital was

....

....

The names of the doctors and midwives who helped us

....

....

....

Memories of your birth day

Now you are really here

People who came to visit us

....

....

....

....

....

Place photo here

A first photo of you

On the day you were born

The weather was ....

A gallon of milk cost ....

The President was ....

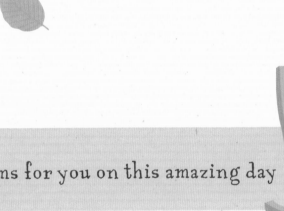

Our thoughts, hopes and dreams for you on this amazing day

....

....

....

....

....

Your first day and night
New experiences for us all

How we slept

You
....

....

Us
....

....

About feeding you
....

....

....

What the doctor and midwife said about you
....

....

....

Gifts, cards and flowers received

Gift	From
....	....
....	....
....	....
....	....
....	....
....	....

Your birth announcement

Place card here

Taking you home
A first introduction to your world

You live at

This is what
your home
looks like

Place photo here

All about the first day and night in your new home

photo of you in your new home

Place photo here

Who you are

Your place in this new world

Your full name

....

Why it was chosen, and why we think it will suit you

....

....

Other names that
we thought about
calling you

....

....

....

This is your family

Great Grandparents

Great Grandparents

Great Grandparents

Great Grandparents

Grandfather

Grandmother

Grandfather

Grandmother

Aunts/Uncles

Daddy

Mommy

Aunts/Uncles

Brothers

You

Sisters

More about your family
special people in your world

	All about Mommy	All about Daddy
Date of birth		
Born in		
Favorite things		
Most looking forward to		

Photo of Mommy and Daddy

Place photo here

Mommy's parents	All about Grandma	All about Grandpa
Name		
Date of birth		
Born in		
Favorite things		

Daddy's parents	All about Grandma	All about Grandpa
Name		
Date of birth		
Born in		
Favorite things		

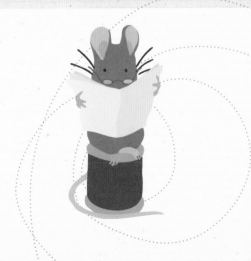

Your early routines
A day in the life of our new arrival

6 am

8 am

10 am

12 pm

2 pm

4 pm

6 pm

8 pm

10 pm

12 am

2 am

4 am

First events
Life is full of exciting experiences

	Date:	Age:
Your first bath		
The first time in your stroller		
Your first trip to the park		
Your first big trip in a car		
The first time we stayed away overnight		

Your first party

....

....

Your first holiday

....

....

A photo from your first holiday

Place photo here

Memorable milestones
Our baby grows more independent

The first time you smiled

Date:

Age:

When you first rolled over

Date:

Age:

Your first laugh, and what it was that made you giggle

Date:

Age:

Your first footprints and handprints

Date: Age:

When you first
slept in your cot

When you first slept
right through the night

Your first tooth

When you first sat up

When you crawled

Things you love
starting to develop your own tastes

Favorite toys

Stories and songs
you love to hear

Food you like best

Favorite games
to play

New friends

Places you love
to visit

Sounds you love
to make

Best furry friends

Discovering more
You are learning new skills

The first sound you made and what we think it meant

The first words you understood

This is the first word you said clearly

....

....

....

....

....

The first time you stood up by yourself

Date: .... Age: ....

....

When you took your first steps you were heading towards

....

....

Going out into the world
You are beginning to grow up

Your first haircut

Date ....

At ....
....

Your first trip to the doctor

Date ....

At ....
....

Immunization	Date

Your height and weight
How you are developing

Date	Age	Height	Weight

Date	Age	Height	Weight

Photo of you
age ....

Place photo here

Memories from your first year

Things you did, things we felt

Your first month

Your second month

Your third month

Your fourth month

....

....

Your fifth month

....

....

Your sixth month

....

....

....

....

....

....

....

Memories from your first year
Things you did, things we felt

Your seventh month

Your eighth month

Your ninth month

Your tenth month

Your eleventh month

Your twelfth month

You are One!

You have had an amazing year

Height

Number of teeth

Words you can say
or are trying to say

Progress towards
crawling and
walking

Handprint
now that
you are
One

Your first birthday

People who celebrated
your first year
with us

....

....

....

Where we were

....

What you wore

....

Presents you
were given

....

....

....

Your birthday cake

....

Songs we sang

....

....

....

Happy Birthday, Baby!

With love to a very special person

Place photo here

Now you are One!

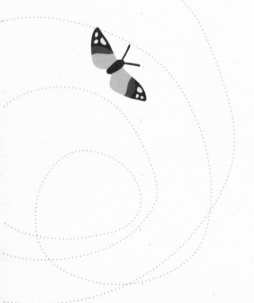